Book Two

NURSERY RHYMES

Illustrated by David Crossley

Brown Watson
ENGLAND

LITTLE MISS MUFFET

Little Miss Muffet
Sat on her tuffet,
Eating her curds and whey;
There came a big spider,
Who sat down beside her,
And frightened Miss Muffet away.

JACK AND JILL

Jack and Jill went up the hill,
To fetch a pail of water;
Jack fell down and broke his crown,
And Jill came tumbling after.

WEE WILLIE WINKIE

Wee Willie Winkie
Runs through the town,
Upstairs and downstairs
In his nightgown.

Rapping at the window,
Crying through the lock,
Are the children all in bed,
For it's past eight o'clock.

PUSSY CAT, PUSSY CAT

Pussy cat, pussy cat,
Where have you been?
I've been up to London,
To visit the Queen.

Pussy cat, pussy cat,
What did you there?
I frightened a little mouse,
Under a chair.

I HAD A LITTLE NUT TREE

I had a little nut tree,
Nothing would it bear
But a silver nutmeg
And a golden pear.

The King of Spain's daughter
Came to visit me,
And all for the sake
Of my little nut tree.

GEORGIE PORGIE

Georgie Porgie, pudding and pie,
Kissed the girls and made them cry;
When the boys came out to play,
Georgie Porgie ran away.

LITTLE JACK HORNER

Little Jack Horner sat in a corner,
Eating his Christmas pie;
He put in his thumb,
And pulled out a plum,
And said "What a good boy am I!"

TWO LITTLE DICKIE BIRDS

Two little dickie birds sitting on a wall,
One named Peter,
One named Paul.

Fly away, Peter!
Fly away, Paul!
Come back, Peter!
Come back, Paul!

PAT-A-CAKE

Pat-a-cake, pat-a-cake, baker's man,
Bake me a cake as fast as you can;
Pat it and prick it and mark it with B,
And put it in the oven for baby and me.

DIDDLE, DIDDLE, DUMPLING

Diddle, diddle, dumpling, my son John,
Went to bed with his trousers on;
One shoe off and one shoe on,
Diddle, diddle, dumpling, my son John.

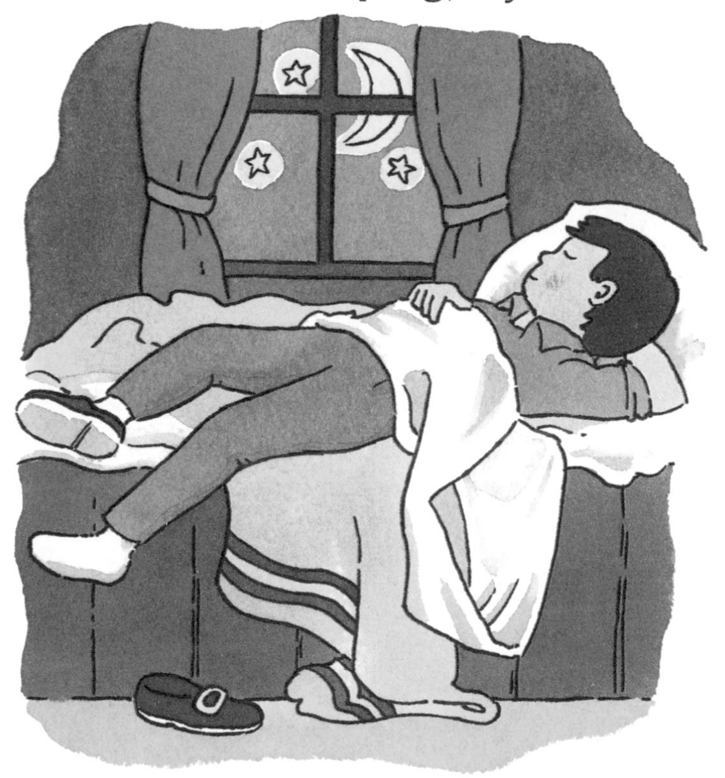

LAVENDER'S BLUE

Lavender's blue, dilly, dilly,
Lavender's green;
When I am King, dilly, dilly,
You shall be Queen.

Call up your men, dilly, dilly,
Set them to work,
Some to the plough, dilly, dilly,
Some to the cart.

Some to make hay, dilly, dilly,
Some to thresh corn,
While you and I, dilly, dilly,
Keep ourselves warm.

TWINKLE, TWINKLE, LITTLE STAR

Twinkle, twinkle, little star,
How I wonder what you are!
Up above the world so high,
Like a diamond in the sky.

HIGGELDY, PIGGELDY

Higgeldy, piggeldy, my black hen,
She lays eggs for gentlemen;
Sometimes nine and sometimes ten,
Higgeldy, piggeldy, my black hen.

THE MAN IN THE MOON

The man in the moon,
Came down too soon,
And asked the way to Norwich.
He went by the south,
And burned his mouth,
By eating cold plum porridge.

TWO LITTLE DUCKS

Two little ducks that I once knew,
Fat ducks, skinny ducks,
There were two.

But the one little duck
With the feathers on his back,
He led the other
With a quack, quack, quack.

THE QUEEN OF HEARTS

The Queen of Hearts
She made some tarts,
All on a summer's day;
The Knave of Hearts
He stole the tarts,
And took them right away.

The King of Hearts
Called for the tarts,
And beat the Knave full sore;
The Knave of Hearts
Brought back the tarts,
And vowed he'd steal no more.

GO TO BED LATE

Go to bed late,
Stay very small;
Go to bed early,
Grow very tall.

A DILLER, A DOLLAR

A diller, a dollar,
A ten o'clock scholar,
What makes you come so soon?
You used to come at ten o'clock,
But now you come at noon.

CURLY LOCKS

Curly Locks, Curly Locks,
Will you be mine?
You shall not wash dishes,
Nor yet feed the swine;